Is It Hot?

Written by
Jill Atkins

Yasmin has a pan.

She has a metal pan.

The metal pan has a lid.

The metal pan is on the gas.

If the gas is on, will the pan get hot? Yes, it will get hot.

If the gas is not on, the pan will not get hot.

Jen is at the tap.

Is it the hot tap?

No, it is not the hot tap.

Jen runs the tap.

The liquid will not get hot.

Is the tap hot?

No, it is not the hot tap.

If the tap is on max, will Jen get a jet of hot liquid?

No, the jet will not be hot.
Jen will not get a jet of hot liquid.

But the liquid will be wet!

Is it hot?

Yes, it is hot.

Is it hot?

Yes, it is hot in the sun. She is hot.

Is Jamal hot?

No, Jamal is not hot. Jamal has a jacket on, but he is not hot.

Is the liquid wax hot?

Yes, the liquid wax is hot.

Is the wax hot?

No, the wax is not hot.

But I bet it will get hot!